Excel 365
The IF Functions

EASY EXCEL 365 ESSENTIALS - BOOK 5

M.L. HUMPHREY

SELECT TITLES BY M.L. HUMPHREY

EXCEL 365 ESSENTIALS
Excel 365 for Beginners
Intermediate Excel 365
102 Useful Excel 365 Functions

EASY EXCEL 365 ESSENTIALS
Formatting
Conditional Formatting
Charts
Pivot Tables
The IF Functions
XLOOKUP Functions

See mlhumphrey.com for Microsoft Word, PowerPoint and Access titles and more

CONTENTS

Introduction

This book is part of the *Easy Excel 365 Essentials* series of titles. These are targeted titles that are excerpted from the main *Excel 365 Essentials* series and are focused on one specific topic.

If you want a more general introduction to Excel, then you should check out the *Excel 365 Essentials* titles instead. In this case, *102 Useful Excel 365 Functions* which covers the various IF functions as well as a number of other functions.

But if all you want is a book that covers this specific topic, then let's continue with a discussion of how to use IF, IFS, COUNTIFS, SUMIFS, AVERAGEIFS, MINIFS, and MAXIFS.

(And, by extension, COUNTIF, SUMIF, and AVERAGEIF.)

The COUNTIFS, SUMIFS, AVERAGEIFS, MINIFS, and MAXIFS Functions

Notation:
COUNTIFS(criteria_range1, criteria1, ...)

SUMIFS(sum_range, criteria_range1, criteria1, ...)

AVERAGEIFS(average_range, criteria_range1, criteria1, ...)

MINIFS(min_range, criteria_range1, criteria1, ...)

MAXIFS(max_range, criteria_range1, criteria1, ...)

Excel Definition:
COUNTIFS: Counts the number of cells specified by a given set of conditions or criteria.

SUMIFS: Adds the cells specified by a given set of conditions or criteria.

AVERAGEIFS: Finds average (arithmetic mean) for the cells specified by a given set of conditions or criteria.

MINIFS: Returns the minimum value among cells specified by a given set of conditions or criteria.

MAXIFS: Returns the maximum value among cells specified by a given set of conditions or criteria.

I'm going to discuss all five of these functions together, because they work in the exact same way. The only difference is what calculation they perform, COUNT, SUM, AVERAGE, MIN, or MAX.

What these functions do is allow you to set one or more criteria that must be met before that value is included in the calculation.

If you want a total of all sales for customers in Texas, that's easy enough to do with SUMIFS.

If you want to know the most that a single customer who bought Blue Whatsits paid (where color and product type are tracked separate), you can get that with MAXIFS.

If you want to compare test scores for male and female students of Professors A and B, you can do that with AVERAGEIFS.

For COUNT, SUM, and AVERAGE there is also a singular option function COUNTIF, SUMIF, and AVERAGEIF. I'm not going to cover those here because they overlap the ones we are going to cover and the inputs are entered in a different order so it can confuse matters. But just keep this in mind if you ever find yourself working with someone who has an older version of Excel that doesn't have the multiple-criteria versions available.

For the criteria input, there are a number of options that you can use, including numbers, text, and cell references.

For numbers, you can either write that as the number (22) or use quote marks around the number ("22"). If you want to use a mathematical expression, like greater than, you have to put that in quotes as well (">22").

For cell references, just use the cell reference (A1).

Text needs to be in quotes ("text"). You can also have criteria for text that aren't exact matches using wildcards, but we'll cover those later in this chapter after we've covered the basics.

Here is our data:

	A	B	C	D	E	F
1	**Customer Last**	**Customer State**	**Product**	**Quantity**	**Price**	**Total**
2	Smith	CA	Whatsits	123	$4.50	$553.50
3	Jones	CA	Whatsits	23	$4.50	$103.50
4	Wong	TX	Whatsits	56	$4.50	$252.00
5	Ramirez	TX	Widgets	12	$120.00	$1,440.00
6	McCormick	CA	Widgets	7	$120.00	$840.00
7	Brady	WA	Widgets	8	$120.00	$960.00

We have six customers who live in various states and bought one of two products in varying quantities. I want to answer the following questions:

- How many customers are located in TX?
- How much have customers from TX spent?
- What is the average transaction for a customer from TX?
- What is the most a customer from TX has spent?
- What is the least a customer from TX has spent?

And here we go:

	A	B	C	D	E	F	G	H	I
9					VALUE	TX			
10							Cell Reference (Cell F9)	Formula	Text	Formula
11	How many customers are located in Texas?					2	=COUNTIFS(B2:B7,F9)	2	=COUNTIFS(B2:B7,"TX")
12	How much have customers from Texas spent?					$1,692.00	=SUMIFS(F2:F7,B2:B7,F9)	$1,692.00	=SUMIFS(F2:F7,B2:B7,"TX")
13	What is the average transaction for a customer from TX?					$846.00	=AVERAGEIFS(F2:F7,B2:B7,F9)	$846.00	=AVERAGEIFS(F2:F7,B2:B7,"TX")
14	What is the most a customer from TX has spent?					$1,440.00	=MAXIFS(F2:F7,B2:B7,F9)	$1,440.00	=MAXIFS(F2:F7,B2:B7,"TX")
15	What is the least a customer from TX has spent?					$252.00	=MINIFS(F2:F7,B2:B7,F9)	$252.00	=MINIFS(F2:F7,B2:B7,"TX")

This is a set of calculations performed on data stored in Cells A2 through F7 where Customer State is stored in Cells B2 through B7 and Total Spent is stored in Cells F2 through F7.

I did the same calculation two ways. Column F uses a cell reference (I put TX in Cell F9). The formula used for each row is shown in Column G.

The other approach put TX into the formula by using quote marks around the text. The results for that one are in Column H and the text of the formulas are in Column I.

For the first question, how many customers are located in Texas, we can use COUNTIFS. These are the two formulas:

$$=COUNTIFS(B2:B7,F9)$$

$$=COUNTIFS(B2:B7,"TX")$$

The COUNTIFS function only requires two inputs, the range that has the values and then the criteria. So the criteria here is either the value in F9 or the value "TX". And that first input B2:B7 is the cell range to look at.

So COUNTIFS goes to Cells B2 through B7 and every time there is TX in the cell, counts that cell. In this case, there are two TX customers, so the result is 2.

For the second question, how much have customers in Texas spent, we can use SUMIFS, because we want to sum their spend.

These are the formulas:

$$=SUMIFS(F2:F7,B2:B7,F9)$$

$$=SUMIFS(F2:F7,B2:B7,"TX")$$

Note here that SUMIFS has three required inputs. There's the cell range to perform the calculation on, Cells F2 through F7 in this case. There's the cell range to look at for the criteria, Cells B2 through B7. And then there's the criteria to use, the value in Cell F9 or TX.

SUMIFS does exactly what COUNTIFS did. It goes to Cells B2 through B7 and finds all of the entries that have TX in them. But then it goes over to Column F for the entries that are a match and it pulls that dollar value. Once it has all of the dollar values, it sums them together and returns a total, $1,692.

AVERAGEIFS, MINIFS, and MAXIFS are identical to SUMIFS in terms of the inputs they require and the process they follow. The only difference is what calculation is performed with the numbers that are captured. So AVERAGEIFS takes the AVERAGE. MINIFS takes the MIN. MAXIFS takes the MAX.

Above, I used a different criteria range and calculation range for SUMIFS, AVERAGEIFS, MAXIFS, and MINIFS. But they can work using the same range for both the criteria and calculation. For example, I could look at the total spent for each customer and sum only those values over $250 using:

$$=SUMIFS(F2:F7,F2:F7,">250")$$

See how the sum range and criteria range are both Cells F2 through F7?

Okay, so that was the most basic use of these functions. One single criteria. And we could have actually used SUMIF, AVERAGEIF, and COUNTIF for those questions. (There are no singular versions for MINIFS and MAXIFS, because they're newer than the other functions.) But the power of the IFS part of these functions is that you are not limited to one criteria for your calculation.

Let's expand this now to questions that include multiple criteria. For the questions below, note that product information is in Column C and quantity purchased is in Column D in our data table.

These are the questions we want to answer:

- How many customers bought more than 50 Whatsits?
- How much did those customers spend?
- What was their average transaction size?
- What is the most one of those customers spent?
- What is the least one of those customers spent?

Here we go:

	A	B	C	D	E	F Result	G	H Formula	I
18						Result		Formula	
19	How many customers bought more than 50 Whatsits?					2		=COUNTIFS(C2:C7,"Whatsits",D2:D7,">50")	
20	How much did those customers spend?					$805.50		=SUMIFS(F2:F7,C2:C7,"Whatsits",D2:D7,">50")	
21	What was their average transaction size?					$402.75		=AVERAGEIFS(F2:F7,C2:C7,"Whatsits",D2:D7,">50")	
22	What is the most one of those customers spent?					$553.50		=MAXIFS(F2:F7,C2:C7,"Whatsits",D2:D7,">50")	
23	What is the least one of those customers spent?					$252.00		=MINIFS(F2:F7,C2:C7,"Whatsits",D2:D7,">50")	

Let's look at the AVERAGEIFS one for this:

$$=AVERAGEIFS(F2:F7,C2:C7,"Whatsits",D2:D7,">50")$$

Same range for the first input, we're still calculating all these values off of the total per customer.

This time, though, our first criteria to apply is in Column C, product type, and we want only transactions for Whatsits. It's a text-based criteria, so we put it in quotes. So far it's pretty much the same as the single-criteria formula examples.

But now we need to add a second criteria using Column D, quantity. To do so, we put a comma and then list our second cell range (D2:D7), and then another comma and list our second criteria that applies to that range (">50").

And so it goes. If you had even more criteria you wanted to apply before you took the average of your values, you'd just add your new criteria range and then the criteria for that range onto the end until you were done adding criteria.

Note that you can mix and match criteria types as much as you want, like I did above with one text-based criteria and one numeric criteria. Have a cell reference for one, text for another, a number for a third, an expression for a fourth. Go wild.

Okay. Now that we have the basics, we need to talk about wildcards for text.

In the examples above, I used "TX". That would only count those entries that had nothing other than TX in the cell. (Or tx in the cell, because it's not case-sensitive.)

Wildcards, however, allow you to make your criteria for text entries fuzzy. (That's my word, not theirs.) Using wildcards, for example, I can write a criteria so that anytime my text is in a cell, Excel will count it, regardless of if there's other text there, too.

The two wildcards are the asterisk (*) and the question mark (?).

An asterisk (*) represents any number of characters or spaces.

So if I use:

=COUNTIFS(C2:C7,"*ts")

that would count all entries in the table where the product name ends in ts. That asterisk allows for any number of characters or spaces before the "ts" but the word has to end there.

In this case, it would count both Widgets and Whatsits. They are different length words that both end in "ts".

You can use multiple asterisks, too. So if I want to count all products with an e in the name, I could do that with:

=COUNTIFS(C2:C7,"*e*")

That's saying there can be any number of characters to the left and any number of characters to the right. All I care about is if there is an e somewhere in that word. (It also works for words that either start with or end with an e because that "any number of characters or spaces" can be zero.)

If you want to limit things more than that and only include words of a certain length or only include words where the position of the text matters, then you can use the question mark (?) instead.

The question mark represents one single character or space.

And it does literally represent a single character or space. So if I have TX in a field and I use a search criteria of "?TX", Excel will not count that TX entry because there is not a space or a character before the TX.

Another example:

$$=COUNTIFS(C2:C7,"Widget?")$$

would count "Widgets", because it has one singular character after Widget. But it would not count "Widgets – Blue" because that has more than one character after Widget.

You can use multiple question marks, too. Just remember that each one represents a single character or space.

What about situations where what you want to search for actually includes an asterisk or a question mark? In those cases include a tilde (~) before the mark to tell Excel to treat it as itself and not a wildcard.

Like so:

$$=COUNTIFS(C2:C7,"Widget~?")$$

This would now look to see if any cell contained the text entry, "Widget?"

Some other tips and tricks.

If you want to use an expression, like >50, but the value you want to use is in a cell, like F9, then what you need to do is write that with the expression in quotes and followed by an ampersand (&) and the cell reference. Like this:

$$=COUNTIFS(D2:D7,">"&B26)$$

This formula will count the number of customers who bought more than fifty of a product where the number 50 is stored in Cell B26.

Also, be sure to test your criteria on edge cases. In this example if I'm looking for "bought more than 50" I'd want to test 49, 50, and 51 to make sure the correct transactions were being captured.

And make sure that if you're using multiple ranges, either for criteria or criteria and calculation, that they are all the same size. If they aren't you'll get a #VALUE! error.

Ranges don't have to be adjacent, but they do have to be the same size. Because behind the scenes, like we saw with SUMPRODUCT, what Excel is actually doing is taking the first value in each criteria range you provide it, determining if the criteria is met for each provided range, and if so taking the first value and setting it aside for the calculation. It then does that with the second and the third and the fourth, etc. until it's done, at which point all of the set aside values are counted, summed, averaged, etc.

Finally, let's discuss some real-world uses of these functions.

I use SUMIFS all the time in my budgeting workbook. I have a calculation of how much I owe for my bills for the month that sums the individual bill amounts but only if I haven't already marked them paid.

I also use SUMIFS in my payment tracking worksheet where I need to sum the amounts I'm owed in different currencies separately and not include any sales where I've already been paid. I have a table with the currency abbreviations and I use a cell reference for the currency value and fix the cell range of what I'm summing using $ signs. That lets me write that formula once and copy it down for all of my currencies. (I then have a conversion rate so I have an approximate idea of how much I'm owed in USD, which is the currency I actually care about.)

And as I mentioned above, if you wanted to look at gender bias or racial bias across different professors, you could set up a data table that looks at the average, max, and min scores for their students. Something like this:

	A	B	C	D	E	F	G	H	I	J	K	L
1	Score	Gender	Professor									
2	67	M	Jones			Smith				Jones		
3	74	M	Jones		AVERAGE	MAX	MIN		AVERAGE	MAX	MIN	
4	89	M	Jones		86.375	92	80	M	78	96	67	
5	70	M	Jones		74	82	70	F	83.8	97	73	
6	72	M	Jones									
7	78	M	Jones		Formula in E4	=AVERAGEIFS($A$2:$A$27,$C$2:$C$27,$E$2,$B$2:$B$27,$H4)						
8	96	M	Jones		Formula in J5	=MAXIFS($A$2:$A$27,$C$2:$C$27,$I$2,$B$2:$B$27,$H5)						
9	89	F	Jones									
10	73	F	Jones									
11	85	F	Jones									
12	97	F	Jones									
13	75	F	Jones									
14	71	F	Smith									
15	78	F	Smith									
16	70	F	Smith									
17	73	F	Smith									
18	70	F	Smith									
19	82	F	Smith									
20	86	M	Smith									
21	86	M	Smith									
22	84	M	Smith									
23	92	M	Smith									
24	89	M	Smith									
25	91	M	Smith									
26	83	M	Smith									
27	80	M	Smith									

In Column A we have a series of test scores for students. In Column B we have the student's gender (I'm just going with M/F here). In Column C we have the Professor.

In Columns E through K and Rows 2 through 4 I have built a table that applies the AVERAGEIFS, MAXIFS, and MINIFS functions to that data based upon the professor and the student gender so that we can easily compare max, min, and average between male and female students for each professor.

I rigged this data so that one of the professors had a clear bias that would show in the results. You can look at the data table and see which one you think it was.

In Rows 7 and 8 I've shared a couple of the formulas I used for this so you can see how you can build a table like this and then fix cell references to make it easier to copy instead of having to redo all your work. Here I could copy down for the male row to the female row without any changes needed, but I did have to change the function that was being used in each column and I did have to change the professor field to complete the right-hand side of the table.

In case you can't see it, here are those two sample functions in the screen shot above:

=AVERAGEIFS($A$2:$A$27,$C$2:$C$27,$E$2,$B$2:$B$27,$H4)

=MAXIFS($A$2:$A$27,$C$2:$C$27,$I$2,$B$2:$B$27,$H5)

It's useful to think about how you can use cell references and tables like this to make your life easier if you're trying to get results across the same data table for multiple values. For example, if I wanted data for each of fifty states, using a table structure like I have above and fixing cell references could save significant time rather than having to change the state value in each formula.

Now that we've covered this set of functions I want to cover the IFS function which is one of my favorite functions.

The IF and IFS Functions

Notation:
IF(logical_test, [value_if_true], [value_if_false])

IFS(logical_test1, value_if_true1,…)

Excel Definition:
IF: Checks whether a condition is met, and returns one value if TRUE, and another value if FALSE.

IFS: Checks whether one or more conditions are met and returns a value corresponding to the first TRUE condition.

The IF function has been around for ages. At its most basic it says, "Look at that cell. IF that cell meets this criteria, THEN return this value, OTHERWISE return that value."

For years I would use "nested IF functions" where instead of the OTHERWISE portion, I'd add another IF function. So it would be, "Look at that cell. IF that cell meets this criteria, THEN return this value, OTHERWISE, IF that cell meets this different criteria, THEN return this other value, OTHERWISE return this third value."

You can nest up to 64 IF functions, which would be insane and probably rife with error. But I would often nest five or six.

The issue with nested IF functions for me was always getting the closing parens in the right place. And if you wrote them from the wrong direction that made it even harder.

But luckily for me and many others, in Excel 2019 they introduced the IFS function, which is built for handling multiple possible outcomes.

The IF function, in my opinion, is still the best choice for binary, either/or situations, and I'll show you why in a moment. But the IFS function is the best choice for situations with three or more possible outcomes.

Either one can be used for all situations we'll look at, and I'll show you that, but it's best if you learn them both.

So. As mentioned above, what these functions do is let you build what I think of as a branching path of outcomes. You start off, and if A is true, you go to the right and get a result. If it's not, you go to the left. On that left-hand path, if B is true, you go to the right and get a result. If it isn't, you go left. And you keep doing this for as many branches as you need.

Maybe a better analogy is that it's like walking down a hallway and opening a door to see if what you're looking for is in that room. Open Door A, if it's there, done, pick up the object on the table. If not, open Door B. If it's there, done. If not, open Door C. You keep going as long as the condition isn't met. Until it is, at which point you get your result, whatever that is.

The result can be a value, like a number or text, as we'll see in our first example, or it can be a calculation as we'll see in one of the more complex examples later.

Basically, these functions are a way to return multiple results using one single function.

Let's just dive in now and look at a few examples and then I'll circle back to putting text to what we're seeing.

I want to start with a basic either/or scenario where we're looking at the day of the week and determining what admissions price to charge, $12.95 for Monday through Friday or $19.95 for Saturday and Sunday:

	A	B	C	D
	Values	Charge	IF Formula	IFS Formula
1	1	$12.95	=IF(A2<6,12.95,19.95)	=IFS(A2<6,12.95,TRUE,19.95)
2	2	$12.95	=IF(A3<6,12.95,19.95)	=IFS(A3<6,12.95,TRUE,19.95)
3	3	$12.95	=IF(A4<6,12.95,19.95)	=IFS(A4<6,12.95,TRUE,19.95)
4	4	$12.95	=IF(A5<6,12.95,19.95)	=IFS(A5<6,12.95,TRUE,19.95)
5	5	$12.95	=IF(A6<6,12.95,19.95)	=IFS(A6<6,12.95,TRUE,19.95)
6	6	$19.95	=IF(A7<6,12.95,19.95)	=IFS(A7<6,12.95,TRUE,19.95)
7	7	$19.95	=IF(A8<6,12.95,19.95)	=IFS(A8<6,12.95,TRUE,19.95)

Column A has our numeric value, 1 through 7, for each day of the week where 1 through 5 are Monday through Friday and 6 and 7 are Saturday and Sunday.

Column B has the results.

Columns C and D have our functions. Column C is the IF function. Column D is the IFS function.

For Row 2, the IF function is:

$$=IF(A2<6,12.95,19.95)$$

And the IFS function is:

$$=IFS(A2<6,12.95,TRUE,19.95)$$

Let's walk through those.

The first "branch" or decision point is asking if the value in Column A is less than 6. (I could have also written that as equal to or less than 5, but I'm dealing with whole numbers and it's easier to just use less than for me.)

If so, the function tells Excel to return the value of 12.95.

That's the first logical test and the first value if true. And it's identical for both of the functions.

$$=IF(A2<6,12.95,$$

$$=IFS(A2<6,12.95,$$

At this point the only difference between the two is the s at the end of if for the IFS function.

Since this is an either/or scenario, the next step is to close the function out.

If the value in that cell *isn't* less than 6, which because we know there are only the seven choices means it's either 6 or 7, we need to tell Excel a different value to return.

With the IF function, we can just list that other value and close the function out, so add:

$$19.95)$$

With the IFS function, because it's built to keep going and going and going, we have to give a second logical test. In this case, because we don't need to go further, that "test" is simply TRUE which essentially means, stop here and return this value. So we add:

$$TRUE,19.95)$$

Once more, here are our final formulas:

$$=IF(A2<6,12.95,19.95)$$

$$=IFS(A2<6,12.95,TRUE,19.95)$$

The difference between the two, for a binary either/or scenario, is that IFS needs to have that TRUE component to work and IF doesn't.

That's why it's easier to use IF for these simple scenarios.

If I wanted to describe the IF function we just wrote in English, I would "read" it this way: IF the value in Cell A2 is less than 6, THEN return 12.95, OTHERWISE return 19.95."

Learning to read IF functions that way makes them easier to write, for me at least. Another trick when they get complex is to draw out the paths you've created.

But for now, let's move on to a more complex scenario where IFS can really shine. Don't be scared when you look at this, we'll walk through it step-by-step.

▲	A	B	C
1	Spend X or More	Get Percent Discount	
2	$25.00	5%	
3	$75.00	10%	
4	$150.00	20%	
5	$250.00	25%	
6			
7	Customer Spend	Cost After Discount	IFS Formula
8	$12.50	$12.50	=IFS(A8<$A$2,A8,A8<$A$3,A8*(1-$B$2),A8<$A$4,A8*(1-$B$3),A8<$A$5,A8*(1-$B$4),TRUE,A8*(1-$B$5))
9	$25.00	$23.75	=IFS(A9<$A$2,A9,A9<$A$3,A9*(1-$B$2),A9<$A$4,A9*(1-$B$3),A9<$A$5,A9*(1-$B$4),TRUE,A9*(1-$B$5))
10	$40.00	$38.00	=IFS(A10<$A$2,A10,A10<$A$3,A10*(1-$B$2),A10<$A$4,A10*(1-$B$3),A10<$A$5,A10*(1-$B$4),TRUE,A10*(1-$B$5))
11	$75.00	$67.50	=IFS(A11<$A$2,A11,A11<$A$3,A11*(1-$B$2),A11<$A$4,A11*(1-$B$3),A11<$A$5,A11*(1-$B$4),TRUE,A11*(1-$B$5))
12	$100.00	$90.00	=IFS(A12<$A$2,A12,A12<$A$3,A12*(1-$B$2),A12<$A$4,A12*(1-$B$3),A12<$A$5,A12*(1-$B$4),TRUE,A12*(1-$B$5))
13	$150.00	$120.00	=IFS(A13<$A$2,A13,A13<$A$3,A13*(1-$B$2),A13<$A$4,A13*(1-$B$3),A13<$A$5,A13*(1-$B$4),TRUE,A13*(1-$B$5))
14	$200.00	$160.00	=IFS(A14<$A$2,A14,A14<$A$3,A14*(1-$B$2),A14<$A$4,A14*(1-$B$3),A14<$A$5,A14*(1-$B$4),TRUE,A14*(1-$B$5))
15	$250.00	$187.50	=IFS(A15<$A$2,A15,A15<$A$3,A15*(1-$B$2),A15<$A$4,A15*(1-$B$3),A15<$A$5,A15*(1-$B$4),TRUE,A15*(1-$B$5))

(Also, let me note here that this scenario may be better handled with a lookup function, but I've always personally disliked those for reasons that may not be true anymore. Don't worry, we'll cover those next and you can decide for yourself. For now…)

What you see here in Cells A1 through B5 is a discount table. If a customer spends $25 or more they get 5% off. If they hit $75 they get 10% off. If they hit $150 they get 20% off. And if they reach $250 or more, 25% off.

It is important when building one of these, and it's a mistake I make often even to this day, that you know when each threshold is triggered. So here it's "spend $25 or more" but sometimes it will be "spend more than $25". Those two scenarios need to be written differently.

That's why in the table of examples in Rows 7 through 15 I've included values that match each discount level. So I can see myself that the formula I wrote works at $25, $75, etc. the way it's supposed to. In this case, that the discount kicks in.

Let's describe what you're seeing in that table in Rows 7 through 15, and then we'll look at the formula.

Column A is the amount the customer spent. Column B is the result of using the IFS function to calculate how much they owe after any discount is applied. Column C is the IFS function that was used.

And, before I deleted it, there was a Column D where I manually went through each of those customer spend amounts, reviewed the table of discounts, and manually calculated what the discount should be to check my results. That column had things like =A15*.75 which is taking the customer spend mount in Cell A15, $250, and multiplying it by 1 minus the discount percent of 25% which is the same as .75.

Always, with something this complex, check your formula independently. Find another way to do the same calculation and make sure that your formula and that other method provide the same result. Once you've done that, you can copy your formula to 100,000 rows and be comfortable that it's working properly.

Writing this I initially had an error I needed to fix and I've been doing this almost thirty years, so never assume you can skip that quality review step.

Okay. Deep breaths. Let's look at the formula in Cell C8:

=IFS(A8<$A$2,A8,A8<$A$3,A8*(1-$B$2),A8<$A$4,A8*(1-$B$3),A8<$A$5,A8*(1-$B$4),TRUE,A8*(1-$B$5))

That's a lot, right? But the beauty of IFS is that you can just chop it starting on the left-hand side and look at each component part. So let's do that. Step one:

=IFS(A8<$A$2,A8,

What that is "saying" is that if the value in Cell A8 (our customer spend amount) is less than the value in Cell A2 (our lowest discount threshold), then just return the value in Cell A8.

There's no discount if we haven't met the first discount tier.

Note here that the A2 is written using dollar signs ($) but the A8 references are not. This is to let me copy the formula to other cells and not have to edit or rewrite it. I want any cell that's in the discount table to be fixed, but all of my customer spend cell references to change.

Also, for me personally, it is easier to go through and do that after I have the whole formula. So I didn't add the dollar signs until the end. But it may be easier for you to do so as you go, because I am probably more prone to miss one the way I do it than someone who adds them as they go.

Next step:

A8<$A$3,A8*(1-$B$2),

Here what this is saying is we already know the value in Cell A8 is equal to or greater than the first discount level in Cell A2. (If that weren't true, we wouldn't be here, we'd already have a result.)

So we know the value is $25 or more. Now we need to know if it's $75 or more. That's what the first portion of the formula is saying. If the customer spend (A8) is less than the next discount level of $75 (in Cell A3), then perform this calculation.

The calculation is taking the customer spend (A8) and multiplying it by 100% minus the discount percent for that first discount tier, 5%, which is in Cell B2.

A few things to note here. We've fixed the reference to the discount table again, $A$3 and $B$2. Also, I have combined two steps with that formula. A8 times 1 minus B2 is the same as A8 minus A8 times B2. You could write it either way, it's going to come down to how your mind works.

And it may be simpler to you to build the table so that you pull the discount percent using the IFS function and then do the math of applying that discount away from the IFS function. In that case, this would be:

A8<$A$3,$B$2,

It would just return the discount percent. And actually that approach follows the "make your assumption visible" rule we discussed at the start. And is less prone to error. Because the error I made when I first wrote this was to forget those parens around 1-$B$2.

But I figured this was also an opportunity to show you that the value Excel returns is not limited to a cell reference. You can have it calculate something for you within the IFS function.

And, finally, the other thing I want to point out here is that the comparison is A8 to A3. We're asking if the value has reached the next discount level. BUT the value we pull is in B2, because we have not reached that next level, so the discount that applies is from Row 2, not Row 3.

This is because of how I structured the discount table and how I'm writing this formula. You could structure either one differently and it would work differently. Always think it through. Ask yourself, *what is this "saying" the way I've written it and so what result does that really mean should be returned here?*

Okay. Step 3 is the same sort of thing again:

A8<$A$4,A8*(1-$B$3),

Same with Step 4:

A8<$A$5,A8*(1-$B$4),

And then we get to the end where someone has spent $250 or more:

TRUE,A8*(1-$B$5))

We tell Excel TRUE to let it know this is where we stop and the result is the final discount percent in the table. Done.

Phew. That was a lot. But you want to see the IF function we would have had to write for this?

=IF(A8<$A$2,A8,IF(A8<$A$3,A8*(1-$B$2),IF(A8<$A$4,A8*(1-$B$3),IF(A8<$A$5,A8*(1-$B$4),A8*(1-$B$5)))))

See all those closing parens at the end? And all those IF functions nested in the middle? And this was the better way to write nested IF functions. There's another way to write them where they don't all close out at the very end, but close out at different points within the formula and it can be a nightmare to track a missing paren.

If you ever find yourself in that sort of situation where you have to see if you properly closed out everything, click into the formula bar for that cell and as you arrow through the formula, Excel will briefly bold both the opening and closing paren that are associated with one another.

The way I structured this one above, by arrowing from the end of the formula, I should see each of those last four parens match up with the beginning of an IF function. If that doesn't happen, chances are I'm missing a closing paren at the end.

It's four closing parens in this scenario because that's the number of IF functions I had to use to write the formula. Here I've bolded each one so you can better see them:

=**IF**(A8<$A$2,A8,**IF**(A8<$A$3,A8*(1-$B$2),**IF**(A8<$A$4,A8*(1-$B$3),**IF**(A8<$A$5,A8*(1-$B$4),A8*(1-$B$5)))))

The other pairs of parens in this formula should be close together. I've tried to bold them below, but it may not show well. Look at (1-$B$2) for an example.

=IF(A8<$A$2,A8,IF(A8<$A$3,A8***(**1-$B$2**)**,IF(A8<$A$4,A8***(**1-$B$3**)**,IF(A8<$A$5,A8***(**1-$B$4**)**,A8***(**1-$B$5**)**))))

You can now forget I ever showed you that, because IFS is the better option. With IFS you can list up to 127 total logical tests and outcomes, but please don't. There are better solutions at that point.

Appendix A: Basic Terminology

These terms are defined in detail in *Excel 365 for Beginners*. This is just a quick overview in case it's needed.

Workbook

A workbook is what Excel likes to call an Excel file.

Worksheet

Excel defines a worksheet as the primary document you use in Excel to store and work with your data. A worksheet is organized into Columns and Rows that form Cells. A workbook can contain multiple worksheets.

Columns

Excel uses columns and rows to display information. Columns run across the top of the worksheet and, unless you've done something funky with your settings, are identified using letters of the alphabet.

The first column in a worksheet will always be Column A. And the number of columns in your worksheet will remain the same, regardless of how many columns you delete, add, or move around. Think of columns as location information that is actually separate from the data in the worksheet.

Rows

Rows run down the side of each worksheet and are numbered starting at 1 and up to a very high number. Row numbers are also locational information. The first row will always be numbered 1, the second row will always be numbered 2, and so on and so forth. There will also always be a fixed number of rows in each worksheet regardless of how many rows of data you delete, add, or move around.

Cells

Cells are where the row and column data comes together. Cells are identified using the letter for the column and the number for the row that intersect to form that cell. For example, Cell A1 is the cell that is in the first column and first row of the worksheet.

Click

If I tell you to click on something, that means to use your mouse (or trackpad) to move the cursor on the screen over to a specific location and left-click or right-click on the option. If you left-click, this selects the item. If you right-click, this generally displays a dropdown list of options to choose from. If I don't tell you which to do, left- or right-click, then left-click.

Left-click/Right-click

If you look at your mouse you generally have two flat buttons to press. One is on the left side, one is on the right. If I say left-click that means to press down on the button on the left. If I say right-click that means press down on the button on the right.

Select

If I tell you to "select" cells, that means to highlight them. You can either left-click and drag to select a range of cells or hold down the Ctrl key as you click on individual cells. To select an entire column, click on the letter for the column. To select an entire row, click on the number for the row.

Data

Data is the information you enter into your worksheet.

Data Table

I may also sometimes refer to a data table or table of data. This is just a combination of cells that contain data in them.

Arrow

If I tell you to arrow to somewhere or to arrow right, left, up, or down, this just means use the arrow keys to navigate to a new cell.

Cursor Functions

The cursor is what moves around when you move your mouse or use the trackpad. In Excel the cursor changes its appearance depending on what functions you can perform.

Tab

I am going to talk a lot about Tabs, which are the options you have to choose from at the top of the workspace. The default tab names are File, Home, Insert, Page Layout, Formulas, Data, Review, View, and Help. But there are certain times when additional tabs will appear, for example, when you create a pivot table or a chart.

(This should not be confused with the Tab key which can be used to move across cells.)

Dropdown Menus

A dropdown menu is a listing of available choices that you can see when you right-click in certain places such as the main workspace or on a worksheet name. You will also see them when you click on an arrow next to or below an option in the top menu.

Dialogue Boxes

Dialogue boxes are pop-up boxes that contain additional choices.

Scroll Bars

When you have more information than will show in a screen, dialogue box, or dropdown menu, you will see scroll bars on the right side or bottom that allow you to navigate to see the rest of the information.

Formula Bar

The formula bar is the long white bar at the top of the main workspace directly below the top menu options that lets you see the actual contents of a cell, not just the displayed value.

Cell Notation

Cells are referred to by their column and row position. So Cell A1 is the cell that's the intersection of the first column and first row in the worksheet.

When written in Excel you just use A1, you do not need to include the word cell. A colon (:) can be used to reference a range of cells. A comma (,) can be used to separate cell references.

When in doubt about how to define a cell range, click into a cell, type =, and then go and select the cells you want to reference. Excel will describe your selection in the formula bar using cell notation.

Paste Special Values

Paste Special Values is a way of pasting copied values that keeps the calculation results or the cell values but removes any formulas or formatting.

Task Pane

On occasion Excel will open a task pane, which is different from a dialogue box because it is part of the workspace. These will normally appear on the right-hand side in Excel for tasks such as working with pivot tables or charts or using the built-in Help function. (They often appear on the left-hand side in Word.)

They can be closed by clicking on the X in the top right corner.

About the Author

M.L. Humphrey is a former stockbroker with a degree in Economics from Stanford and an MBA from Wharton who has spent close to twenty years as a regulator and consultant in the financial services industry.

You can reach M.L. at mlhumphreywriter@gmail.com or at mlhumphrey.com.

* * *

If you want to learn more about Microsoft Excel, check out *Excel Tips and Tricks* or one of the main Excel 365 Essentials titles, *Excel 365 for Beginners, Intermediate Excel 365,* or *102 Useful Excel 365 Functions.*

www.ingramcontent.com/pod-product-compliance
Lightning Source LLC
Chambersburg PA
CBHW082106070326
40689CB00054B/4743